P9-CFF-230

COLONIZATION AND SETTLEMENT
IN THE NEW WORLD: 1585–1763

by Pat McCarthy

Content Consultant
Edward M. Cook Jr.
Associate Professor of History
University of Chicago

CORE
LIBRARY

Published by ABDO Publishing Company, PO Box 398166, Minneapolis, MN 55439. Copyright © 2014 by Abdo Consulting Group, Inc. International copyrights reserved in all countries. No part of this book may be reproduced in any form without written permission from the publisher. The Core Library™ is a trademark and logo of ABDO Publishing Company.

Printed in the United States of America,
North Mankato, Minnesota
102013
012014

Editor: Lauren Coss
Series Designer: Becky Daum

Library of Congress Control Number: 2013913121

Cataloging-in-Publication Data
McCarthy, Pat.
 Colonization and settlement in the New World: 1585-1763 / Pat McCarthy.
    p. cm. -- (The story of the United States)
Includes bibliographical references and index.
ISBN 978-1-62403-172-4
1. United States--History--Colonial period, ca. 1600-1775--Juvenile
literature. 2. United States--Social life and customs--To 1775--Juvenile
literature. 3. United States--Social life and customs--Juvenile literature. I.
Title.
973.2--dc23

                                                    2013913121

Photo Credits: North Wind Picture Archives/AP Images, cover, 1; North Wind/North Wind Picture Archives, 4, 7, 11, 14, 19, 22, 25, 28, 33, 34, 37, 39, 45; Red Line Editorial, 9; PoodlesRock/Corbis, 17; Francis G. Mayer/Corbis, 31; Jackson Walker/National Guard Image Gallery, 40

Cover: Pilgrims from Great Britain arrive to found the Plymouth Colony in what is now Massachusetts.

CONTENTS

CHAPTER ONE

HERE TO STAY

For thousands of years, up to the 1500s, North America was largely unexplored by Europeans. As Europeans became aware of this huge, faraway continent, many referred to North America as the New World. Explorers from Europe had been visiting the New World since Vikings arrived in modern-day Canada in approximately 1000 CE. Explorers from

In approximately 1000 CE, Scandinavian Vikings were the first European colonists to arrive in the New World.

other European countries, including Portugal, Spain, France, and Great Britain, began arriving in the 1400s.

In the 1500s, Spain was building an empire in North and South America. This empire soon became very profitable. In 1565 Spain set up the outpost of Saint Augustine in what is now Florida. This was the first permanent European settlement in what would become the United States. By the late 1500s, more Europeans had arrived in the New World. Several European countries hoped to set up colonies. They hoped to match Spain's success. Having colonies gave a country more resources and power. Colonizing countries hoped to get gold, silver, furs, and other valuable items from North America.

The First Colonies

By the 1580s, Great Britain was eager to establish its own colonies in North America. But early British colony attempts failed. In 1606 King James I gave the Virginia Company of London a charter. The king's charter was a document giving land rights in North

Native Americans traded furs with early European explorers. Other interactions between Europeans and Native Americans were not so peaceful.

America to the Virginia Company. Any land the Virginia Company claimed would belong to the king. The Virginia Company would help manage the land for him. Virginia Company men arrived in what is now Virginia on April 26, 1607.

The men aboard the ships chose a site about 20 miles (32 km) up from a river to build their settlement. They named the settlement Jamestown, after the king. It was located on a peninsula, with water on three sides. The men built a three-sided wooden fort. They began looking for the gold and silver deposits they believed were common throughout the New World.

Troubles at Jamestown

The Jamestown colonists faced many challenges from the beginning. Approximately 50,000 Native Americans lived in hundreds of small villages throughout the area. Gold and silver were not common in Virginia. But some settlers believed Native Americans knew the locations of gold and silver deposits and simply refused to share the information. Native Americans were not always willing to give up their land to the new settlers. Some tribes attacked the colony. Skirmishes between Native Americans and colonists resulted in several deaths on each side during the first few months after the settlers arrived.

The Jamestown Colony also faced frequent food shortages. Most of the first settlers were not planning to farm. They hoped to get food and resources by

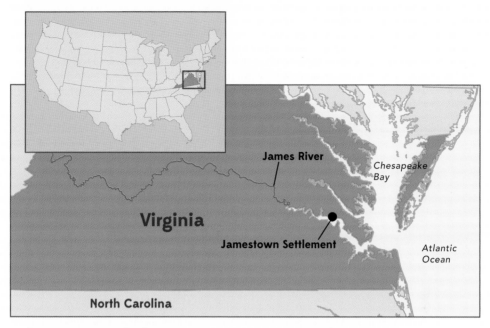

Jamestown Colony

This map shows the location of the Jamestown Colony. Compare this map to the information about the colony you learned in this chapter. Why might this location have been a good place to found a settlement? What might be some drawbacks of settling at this site?

trading with Native Americans. Other food supplies were to be brought from Great Britain. But the Native Americans often did not have enough food to feed their own people. They could not spare any extra for the settlers.

When the Native Americans would not trade, the Jamestown settlers took food by force. This led to more conflicts. In May 1610, more settlers arrived with

Powhatan

Powhatan was an important Native-American leader at the time Jamestown Colony was settled. He led an alliance of Algonquian-speaking Native-American tribes. Powhatan's empire was called *Tsenacommacah* in the Algonquian language, but its people became known as the Powhatan, after their leader. At one point, Powhatan ruled more than 14,000 people. In 1614 colonist John Rolfe married Powhatan's daughter Pocahontas. Relations between the settlers and the Native Americans improved because of the marriage.

supplies. Jamestown's leaders began focusing more on farming so they could support the colony without trading. Farming required more land, which the settlers took from the Native Americans. Conditions in the colony began improving. More settlers arrived.

Peace and Tobacco

In 1612 Jamestown settler John Rolfe began growing tobacco. Jamestown now had a new crop it could sell to Great Britain to help support the colony. Rolfe's tobacco grew well in Virginia. But it took a great deal of work to farm. In 1619 a ship arrived in Jamestown carrying

Tobacco became an important crop in Jamestown Colony. The settlers sold the tobacco to Great Britain.

approximately 20 African slaves. The slaves had been kidnapped from their homes in Africa and taken to North America. The ship's captain traded the slaves to Jamestown colonists for supplies. The Africans worked in Jamestown's tobacco fields. Some historians believe these early African slaves were more like indentured servants. This means they would

Indentured Servants

Indentured servants were common in the early American colonies. In most cases, these people had their passage across the Atlantic paid for by a master. In exchange, the indentured servant worked for the master for a period of time. Servants received food and a place to live. But they were not paid for their work. After they completed their time of service, indentured servants were free. The indentured servant system allowed landowners to build the labor force needed to work in farm fields.

be freed after working a certain number of years.

That same year, the General Assembly of Virginia was created. This group of elected male landowners led the colony. The colonists remained under the control of the British king. But they were now allowed to make laws for themselves. In 1624 the British king made Jamestown and the settlements around it an official British colony, called Virginia. Jamestown was its capital. The colony no longer belonged to the Virginia Company. The king now managed it.

In 1607 Jamestown settler George Percy described the harsh conditions of the colony in his journal:

> Our men were destroyed with cruel diseases, as Swellings, Fluxes, Burning Fevers, and by wars, but for the most part they died of mere famine. . . . There were never Englishmen left in a foreign Country in such misery as we were in this new discovered Virginia. . . . Our food was but a small Can of Barley sod in water, to five men a day, our drink cold water taken out of the River, which was at a flood very salty, at a low tide full of slime and filth, which was the destruction of many of our men. Thus we lived for the space of five months in this miserable distress. . . . it pleased God after a while to send [the Virginia Indians] which were our mortal enemies to relieve us with . . . bread, corn, fish, and flesh in great plenty.

Source: George Percy. Jamestown: 1607, the First Months. London: George Percy, 1608. National Humanities Center, 2006. Web. Accessed August 15, 2013.

Consider Your Audience

Read this passage carefully. An adult colonist wrote this journal entry more than 400 years ago. Think about what it means. How would you write the same information for a modern audience, such as your friends? Write a blog post conveying this information to the new audience.

CHAPTER TWO

FOR FREEDOM AND PROFIT

With Jamestown finally prospering, other British citizens were eager to settle in the New World. In 1620 a new group of settlers arrived in North America on the ship the *Mayflower*. Unlike the first Jamestown colonists, these settlers were not looking for riches and resources. They were seeking religious freedom.

The settlers who crossed the Atlantic Ocean on the Mayflower hoped to find religious freedom in the New World.

The First Thanksgiving

In the fall of 1621, the Pilgrims and Wampanoag shared a harvest feast. The feast lasted three days. Approximately 50 colonists and 90 Wampanoag attended. The Native Americans brought deer meat. The colonists provided birds they had hunted. Turkey may have been one of the birds.

Settling Massachusetts

The new settlers were known as Pilgrims. They had separated from the Church of England and faced persecution in Great Britain as a result. In December the *Mayflower* landed at Plymouth in what is now Massachusetts. It was a difficult winter for the Pilgrims. Half of the 102 people who had arrived on the *Mayflower* died before spring.

Like Jamestown, the Plymouth area was home to many Native-American tribes. In March the Pilgrims met two English-speaking Native Americans, Samoset and Squanto. Squanto introduced the settlers to Chief Massasoit of the Wampanoag tribe. Eventually the settlers and Native Americans signed a peace

In 1621 the Pilgrims and Native Americans celebrated with a harvest feast.

treaty, which lasted more than 50 years. The Native Americans helped teach the Pilgrims to farm and survive in their new home. Four shiploads of settlers arrived in the next six years. Settlers began spreading to the region around Plymouth.

With Plymouth a success, more British settlers flooded into New England. In 1630 another religious group came to New England in search of religious freedom. They were Puritans, a religious group that wanted to reform the Church of England. The Puritans started the Massachusetts Bay Colony under a royal charter from King Charles I.

More Colonies

While British colonists were seeking religious freedom in Massachusetts, another group of colonists wanted to set up colonies in New England to make money. Settlers arrived in what is now New Hampshire in 1623. They hoped to establish a fishing colony.

Holland also wanted to build colonies in New England. The Dutch West India Company was especially interested in North America. In 1609 explorer Henry Hudson claimed the land between the Delaware and Connecticut Rivers for Holland. The claim was known as New Netherland. The Dutch West India Company's goal was to build permanent colonies in New Netherland. It planned to make money from the fur trade.

In 1624 the Dutch built a fort on Manhattan Island off the coast of what is now New York. The area

Henry Hudson

was home to the Algonquian people. The Dutch traded with the Algonquian for furs, which they sold to people in Europe. In 1626 the Dutch West India Company sent Peter Minuit to be the governor of New Netherland. Minuit named the settlement New Amsterdam and waited for more settlers to arrive. Later the settlement would pass into British hands, becoming part of New York.

Colonizing Maryland

In 1632 King Charles I gave Cecilius Calvert, known as Lord Baltimore, a charter to set up a colony in what is now Maryland. Three hundred settlers arrived in Maryland in March 1634. They paid the Native Americans for the land with axes, tools, and cloth.

Freedom of Religion

The Calverts were Roman Catholics, but they wanted the colony open to all Christian religions. Many settlers coming to Maryland were Protestants. In 1649 the colony passed the Maryland Toleration Act. This guaranteed religious freedom to all Christians in Maryland.

The colony grew quickly. The colonists' relationships with the Native Americans were mostly friendly. The land was fertile, and the climate was mild. Maryland's biggest crop was tobacco. In 1639 enslaved Africans were brought to the area to help with the tobacco crop.

In November 1620, the *Mayflower* travelers crafted a document known as the Mayflower Compact before leaving the ship and going ashore. This became the foundation of Plymouth's government:

> *In the name of God, Amen. We whose names are under-written. . . . solemnly and mutually, in the presence of God, and one of another, covenant and combine our selves together into a civil body politic, for our better ordering and preservation and furtherance of the ends aforesaid; and by virtue hereof to enact, constitute, and frame such just and equal laws, ordinances, acts, constitutions and offices, from time to time, as shall be thought most meet and convenient for the general good of the Colony, unto which we promise all due submission and obedience. In witness whereof we have hereunder subscribed our names at Cape Cod, the eleventh of November. . . . Anno Dom. 1620.*

Source: "Text of the Mayflower Compact." Beyond the Pilgrim Story. *Pilgrim Hall Museum*, 2012. Web. Accessed August 14, 2013.

What's the Big Idea?

Read this passage carefully. Ask an adult to help you look up any words you don't know. What are the *Mayflower* passengers' main goals in this document? How do they plan to accomplish these goals?

CHAPTER THREE

SETTLEMENTS EXPAND

By the 1630s, British colonists had a better idea of how to survive in the New World. They needed a steady supply of food from farming or Native-American trade. They needed some sort of colonial government. And they needed to sell goods, such as food, furs, and timber, to make money.

Soon growing colonies dotted the eastern coast of North America. Puritan minister Thomas

Puritan leader Thomas Hooker and his followers built the first Connecticut Colony settlement on land they bought from local Native Americans.

Hooker established the first permanent settlement in Connecticut Colony in 1636. Hooker brought settlers from Massachusetts to live in his colony.

Connecticut Colony

Settlers continued arriving at Connecticut Colony. The settlers expanded further into Pequot territory. The Pequot were a group of Native Americans who lived in the region surrounding Connecticut Colony.

In 1637 the colonists and the Pequot went to war. The colonists won, and most of the Pequot who had survived the war left the region. With no

The Pequot War

In 1637 a group of Pequot began attacking settlements near Hartford, Connecticut. In May Captain John Mason led a group of approximately 70 men to attack the Pequot. The River and Mohegan peoples were enemies of the Pequot. They agreed to help the colonists. The colonists and their Native-American allies completely destroyed the main Pequot village. More than 500 Pequot were killed. Many survivors left the area. Other surviving Pequot were given to other Native-American tribes as slaves.

Few Pequot remained in Connecticut Colony after the 1637 war against the colonists.

more Pequot resistance, Connecticut continued expanding. In 1639 men from three Connecticut villages, Hartford, Wethersfield, and Windsor, met to establish a government for the area. Representatives from each village worked to create a document known as the Fundamental Orders of Connecticut. This laid out guidelines for governing the three villages.

Some historians consider this document to be the first constitution in America.

Rhode Island, Delaware, and New Jersey

While Connecticut colonists were building settlements, colonies continued to spring up along the Atlantic coast. People breaking off from other colonies started many of these new colonies. In 1636 Roger Williams brought a group of settlers to what became Rhode Island Colony. Williams had been banished from the Massachusetts Bay Colony the year before because of his beliefs. He believed the government should

---

The Colonies Unite

In 1643 several northeastern colonies joined together to form the New England Confederation. They thought it would help solve problems of boundaries, trade, and religious disagreements. More importantly it would give them a unified defense against attacks by the Dutch, the French, and Native Americans.

EXPLORE ONLINE

One of the focuses in Chapter Three is the Pequot War. The Web site at the link below also discusses the Pequot War. How is the information in the Web site different from the information in the chapter? What information is the same? What can you learn from this Web site?

Pequot War

www.mycorelibrary.com/colonization-and-settlement

not support or control churches. Williams supported religious freedom for all—not just Christians.

In 1664 the British took over New Netherland. It became New York, Delaware, and New Jersey. Sir George Carteret and Lord Berkeley shared ownership of New Jersey. They drew up a constitution called the Concessions and Agreements for New Jersey in 1664. The colony still answered to the British king. But this was the beginning of self-government in the colony.

CHAPTER FOUR

TROUBLES AND SUCCESSES

By 1671 New England colonists outnumbered the Native Americans in the area. Wampanoag chief Metacom, whom the colonists called King Philip, was determined to push the colonists off his tribe's land. He persuaded other Native-American tribes to join his efforts.

In 1675 the tensions between colonists and Native Americans erupted into war.

King Philip's War

In 1675 war broke out across New England. Approximately 3,000 Native Americans and 600 colonists were killed in the fighting. Entire Native-American tribes were destroyed. Many Native Americans who escaped capture moved farther north or west after the war ended in 1676. Wars with Native Americans still broke out along New England's northern and western borders. But few Native Americans remained in the heart of the colonies. Native Americans began seeking support from France, which claimed Canada.

Pennsylvania

British settlements continued expanding in the Northeast. In 1681 Great Britain's King Charles II granted land to a Quaker named William Penn. The land was part of the original New Netherland region. Penn named his colony Pennsylvania.

Penn arrived in 1682 and built a town called Philadelphia. The city grew quickly. After three years,

William Penn established mostly positive relationships with the Native Americans in Pennsylvania.

it was home to 2,500 colonists. Pennsylvania quickly became one of the strongest colonies.

The Carolinas

While settlers were busy expanding the northern settlements, new colonies were also cropping up along the southern Atlantic Coast. In 1663 King Charles II gave eight lords a section of land along the Atlantic Coast. The lords used the land to form a new colony called Carolina. They formed a settlement in southern Carolina in 1670. The settlement was called Charles Town, for the king. Charles Town became the capital of Carolina.

Settling South Carolina

Charles Town settlers came from all over the world. Many European settlers came from islands in the Caribbean. Some of these settlers owned large plantations with slaves. They set up new plantations in Carolina. Many African people were brought to the region against their will to work as slaves. As the demand for rice and other crops grew, colonists acquired more slaves. By 1708 African slaves outnumbered Carolina's white settlers.

The southern part of Carolina grew much faster than the northern part. Most of the settlers in the northern part came from Virginia. Many owned small farms and only a few slaves. Southern settlers often came from across the globe. Many owned large plantations. These plantations relied on slave labor. People were generally much wealthier in southern Carolina.

South Carolina's many plantations allowed the colony to become wealthier than its northern neighbor.

In 1719 the king bought Carolina back from the proprietors. The northern and southern settlements in Carolina were far from one another. The two parts of the colony had developed independently. In 1729 Carolina became two separate colonies, North Carolina and South Carolina.

CHAPTER FIVE

THE FINAL COLONY AND WAR

Georgia was the last British colony settled. At the time in Great Britain, people who could not pay their debts were often thrown in prison. British leader James Oglethorpe wanted to give debtors a new life in North America. In 1732 King George II, who had become king of Great Britain in 1727, granted a charter to Oglethorpe. The charter allowed

James Oglethorpe chose the site where Savannah, Georgia, stands today to begin his settlement. He bought land from the Native Americans in the area.

Defending South Carolina

King George II had good reason for granting Oglethorpe the charter to start Georgia. South Carolina had become very successful. But it was dangerously close to Spanish territory. The Spanish still controlled Florida, Mexico, and much of the Caribbean. Great Britain feared Spain would try to take control of South Carolina. Oglethorpe's colony would help protect South Carolina from the Spanish.

Oglethorpe to start a colony for debtors on the land south of Carolina.

Settling Georgia

In 1732 Oglethorpe and a shipload of settlers sailed for the land that would become Georgia. The settlers came from many places and backgrounds. All religions except Catholics were welcome. Oglethorpe named his colony Georgia, after the king. The settlers cleared the land, built houses, and planted crops and gardens. Both Native Americans and people from South Carolina helped provide food for the new settlers.

Oglethorpe began preparing to defend Georgia from a possible attack from Spain. In 1738, 700 troops

In 1740 Oglethorpe and his men attempted to capture Spain's Saint Augustine settlement, but the attack failed.

arrived from Great Britain. Oglethorpe recruited 1,000 Native Americans to help him if the Spanish attacked. In 1742 the Spanish invaded Georgia. Oglethorpe's men fought back. They won a bloody battle on Saint Simons Island, off the coast of Georgia. The Spanish did not attempt another invasion.

In 1749 slavery became legal in Georgia. Colonists began growing crops, such as rice and indigo. These crops required a great deal of labor. Georgia also had a thriving lumber industry.

Discontent among Settlers

By the early 1700s, colonial assemblies governed all the colonies, except Georgia. The colonists elected representatives to these assemblies. The assemblies made laws for each of their colonies. Georgia, on the other hand, was led by a group of trustees who lived in Great Britain. Georgia's colonists had no power in their colony's government. The trustees made strict rules for the new colony. Slavery and alcohol were banned in the colony. Each colonist was only allowed to own 500 acres (202 ha) of land. Many people were unhappy with the colony's rules.

French and Indian War

By the 1750s, Great Britain had a firm hold on the East Coast of the future United States. But two other major European countries still claimed ownership of North America. The Spanish owned Florida, Mexico, and parts of the Caribbean. France claimed Canada and the Ohio River Valley west of the Appalachian Mountains. However, the British also claimed the Ohio River Valley.

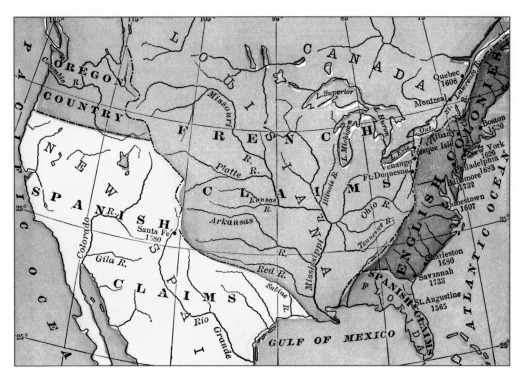

North America before the French and Indian War
This map shows the way North America was divided in the 1750s. How does this map help you better understand the circumstances that led to British conflicts with Spain and France? Why do you think both France and Great Britain were so eager to settle the Ohio River Valley?

The French and the British continued disputing which country owned the land. In 1754 the dispute erupted into war between the two nations. The North American conflict became known as the French and Indian War (1754–1763). Many Native Americans fought with the French. The British had pushed many

The French and Indian War was part of the conflict between France and Great Britain known as the Seven Years' War, which took place from 1756 to 1763.

of these tribes off their land. The Native Americans expected the French would treat them better if they won. However, some tribes fought on behalf of the British. The war between Great Britain and France also raged in Europe, where it became known as the Seven Years' War.

The fall of Montreal, Canada, to the British in 1760 marked the end of the war in the colonies. The Treaty of Paris, signed in 1763, granted the British control of Canada and most of the land east of the Mississippi River.

It seemed as if the British were poised to take over all of North America. But some colonists had other ideas. They dreamed of becoming independent from King George and British rule.

IMPORTANT DATES

1607

Jamestown, Virginia, becomes the first permanent colony in the New World.

1620

Plymouth is the first permanent colony in Massachusetts.

1624

The Dutch start the first permanent settlement in what is now New York.

1670

Charles Town is founded in southern Carolina.

1675

King Philip's War begins in New England.

1682

William Penn founds Pennsylvania.

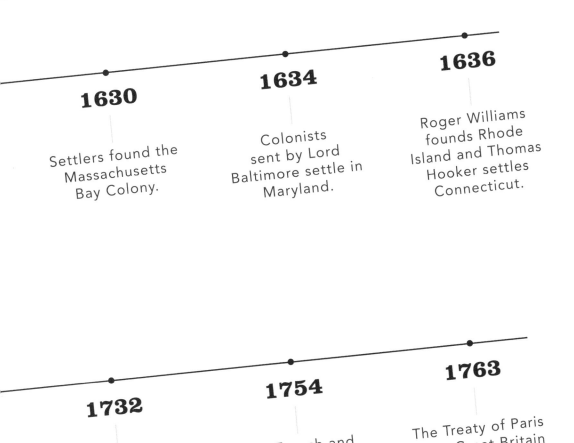

1630

Settlers found the Massachusetts Bay Colony.

1634

Colonists sent by Lord Baltimore settle in Maryland.

1636

Roger Williams founds Rhode Island and Thomas Hooker settles Connecticut.

1732

James Oglethorpe founds Georgia.

1754

The French and Indian War begins.

1763

The Treaty of Paris gives Great Britain control of French land in North America.

STOP AND THINK

Why Do I Care?

The events discussed in this book happened hundreds of years ago. But there are still similarities between your life and the way early colonists lived. How does colonial American history affect your life today? How might your life be different if colonists hadn't settled where they did?

You Are There

Chapter Two of this book discusses the settlement of Plymouth Colony. Imagine you are a child traveling on the *Mayflower*. How do you feel about leaving your home in Great Britain? Are you afraid? What are you most excited to see?

Tell the Tale

Chapter One of this book talks about indentured servants. Write a story about the experiences of an indentured servant in Jamestown Colony. Make sure to set the scene, develop a sequence of events, and write a conclusion.

Surprise Me

Learning about US history can be interesting and surprising. After reading this book, what three facts about colonization did you find most surprising? Write a few sentences about each of those facts. Why did they surprise you?

GLOSSARY

banish
force to permanently leave a place

debtor
a person who owes money

indigo
a plant from which blue dye is made

persecuted
treated poorly because of a person's religion or race

plantation
a large farm that grows one main crop, such as cotton, rice, or tobacco

proprietors
owners

Quaker
a member of a Christian religious group that is against war and prefers simple religious services

reform
to change something for the better

treaty
a formal agreement between two groups or nations

trustee
someone who has been given the authority to govern something

LEARN MORE

Books

Hamen, Sue E. *The Thirteen Colonies*. Minneapolis: ABDO, 2013.

Hermes, Patricia. *Our Strange New Land: Elizabeth's Jamestown Colony Diary*. New York: Scholastic, 2002.

Web Links

To learn more about colonization and settlement in the New World, visit ABDO Publishing Company online at **www.abdopublishing.com**. Web sites about colonization are featured on our Book Links page. These links are routinely monitored and updated to provide the most current information available. Visit **www.mycorelibrary.com** for free additional tools for teachers and students.

INDEX

ABOUT THE AUTHOR

Pat McCarthy is a former elementary school teacher who has written many children's books. She is very interested in history, nature, and biographies. She lives in Ohio with her two cats, Shelby and Whiskers.